Beginning with God

I0200277

Navigating the inevitable processes of life's journey

Book One of the Duncan-Williams Youth Series

Archbishop Nicholas Duncan-Williams

A GOSHEN PUBLISHERS PAPERBACK   VIRGINIA

Beginning with God
Navigating the inevitable processes of life's journey
Book One

ISBN: 978-0-9994003-7-1

Published in 2019
by:

GOSHEN PUBLISHERS LLC
P.O. Box 1562
Stephens City, Virginia, USA
www.GoshenPublishers.com

Our books may be purchased in bulk for promotional, educational, or business use. Please email Agents@GoshenPublishers.com.

First Edition 2019

Cover designed by Goshen Publishers LLC

The Duncan-Williams Youth Series seeks, among several others, to bless you in the following ways:

1. Help you totally yield your life and your future to God, trusting and depending wholly on Him;

2. Equip and challenge you to build and maintain a vibrant intimate relationship with God so you can navigate the journey of life more decisively;

3. Help you become a man or woman of prayer, drawing power from your fellowship with God to deal with situations in your life;

4. Get you to pay closer attention to the

value of the family of God on earth, so you can stay with the brethren and not become an easy target of the enemy;

5. Help you identify sin in its forms and resolve to confront sin with the principles and power of God;

6. Dare you to be different in your generation that is heavily influenced by immorality and godlessness, and thereby walk in integrity, honoring God in your life always;

7. Assist you to discover and develop your God-given talents and spiritual gifts by which you can offer acceptable service in the house of God;

8. Help you develop Christian character as

the foundation for a future life of

leadership and purpose;

9. Challenge you to share your faith in

   Christ as per the gospel, and God's

   power unto salvation without fear, and

   become a good evangelist for God;

10. Help you know how to draw strength

    from the Holy Spirit, stand in the

    position of authority, and walk in victory

    in all the issues confronting you as a

    growing person; and

11. Help you understand and develop

    healthful habits in relating with the

    opposite sex, and thereby prepare for a

    meaningful marriage and family life.

BEGINNING WITH GOD

Book One

Navigating the inevitable processes
of life's journey

Other publications in this series:

- ✓ Book 2: *Becoming a Strong Christian*
- ✓ Book 3: *Developing Intimacy with God*
- ✓ Book 4: *Setting Yourself Apart unto God*
- ✓ Book 5: *Discovering and Walking in Purpose*

All by Archbishop Nicholas Duncan-Williams

This book belongs to

_____

[Name]

Contents

Duncan-Williams Youth Series: Book One

INTRODUCTION

When you are a child, becoming an adult looks far away. In fact, most young, growing people do not have a future paradigm. In other words, the concept of the future is not a critical part of their thinking. They live in the now and focus on what they see today.

Young people also tend to hop from one place to another in search of what excites them most. What looks exciting today becomes boring tomorrow. In the process, their focus continues to shift from one thing to another.

When you meet your classmate or a friend and ask, "What's up?" What answers do you receive? Most of the answers you receive, as well as what you also give to those who ask you that question, point to what's happening now. "Nothing much," or "It's all good," are some of the responses, and they are all about what is currently happening.

Very few young people talk about the future. They talk about what is happening now, and how to get involved so they can be identified as being "in". Young people normally do not want to be left out of today's show. They think they find happiness in what's going on now. Indeed, they get the excitement they are looking for, only that it is temporal and does not last.

Is it not time for the youth to move away from living only for the present and develop a forward-thinking mindset?

The futuristic paradigm simply states that the **future starts today.** It will be helpful for you if, as a young person, you personalize it and say to yourself, "My future starts today."

An expanded declaration for you could be as follows:

There is a future waiting ahead of me. It often appears to be far away, but I know now, that it is closer than it appears.

Actually, I am responsible for its creation. I no longer live in the old paradigm that says life is here today, let us have all we can. My declaration is that there is a future out there and it starts today. It does not start in a vacuum. It starts when I start it and totally commit to it.

I start my future with the choices I make today. I will be certain to make the right choices today, so I can birth my future. In Jesus' name, Amen!

The immediate implication for this truth is that everything you do today is creating a certain future for you. Most of the time, the things we do seem little and insignificant; yet, these little things are the very things creating the future we want. We may not be conscious that we are creating our future; yet, the reality remains unchanged, that we are creating it.

If you skip classes for something else, you are creating a future of irresponsibility. If you waste all the money your parents give you on frivolous things, you are creating a future of reckless living. If you cannot control your sexual urges and live in abstinence, you are creating a future of infidelity when you marry. If you cannot be honest in your dealings today, you are creating a future of fraud and corruption. If you learn to understand people and respect them today, you are creating a future of healthy relationships. If you work hard and wait for the results of your hard work, you are creating a future of entrepreneurship. That is how it works.

So, you see that anything you do today is very closely linked with what you will become in the future.

If someone asks you what you are planning to become in the future, what answers are you ready to give?

If all young people, including you, accept the paradigm of the future, it will change their thought patterns, their attitudes, their behaviors, and their overall lifestyle beginning today.

If you, as a young person, project your life into the future, you should see a prescribed sequence of landmarks that seem to follow an order. Violating that order could lead to all kinds of unpleasant experiences and, possibly, an unpleasant future.

Many adults did not ask the important questions when they were growing up, so they made decisions and choices that were not informed by lasting biblical foundations. Decisions were made in the spur of the moment, which always resulted in future inconsistencies.

Life must always start with the future. This means that you take a mental leap and decide what you want to see for yourself in the future. When that has been clearly perceived, you can then spend the rest of your life working to achieve it.

God asked Abraham to look out and as far as he could see, God would give it to him. God was asking Abraham, even at that age, to look as far as he could see.

As a young person, practice looking farther away from today to see what is out there for you. Determine, with the guidance of the Holy Spirit, to paint a mental picture of your future. You don't build your future when you get there. You build it today and then you get there.

You start building your future from today. It is not something that will happen automatically. It must be made to happen. The singular person that will cause it to happen is you. All others around you are either helping you get to where you have envisaged you are going or pulling you back to where you are. The decision to propel yourself into the future rests with you.

God is ever ready to help you make that critical decision to craft your future according to His purposes for your life.

In this first publication of my *Duncan-Williams Youth Series*, I will introduce you to the inevitable stages everyone goes through in life and how to approach them to be blessed.

I want you to understand the stages that we all go through. The way one approaches these determines to a large extent how one's life turns out. Some of the stages are beyond your control, but a lot of them are within your reach and your input and, therefore, become very critical.

This book explains the stages of life for everyone.

1.

ENTERING THIS WORLD

Once upon a time, your mother carried you in her womb for nine months and then gave birth to you. You had no choice over this one. Your parents gave you a name and took care of you. You had no choice in those matters either, even though you were born with the power of choice. They fed you, bathed you, got you to sleep, and woke you up when they felt like it. In those early years of your life you hardly made any decisions.

You did not decide who your parents would be, where they would come from, and their social and cultural backgrounds. Like Adam, you awakened and realized a wide wonderful world around you, which you had no part in creating. That is the case with this first stage of your life.

If you happen to have good parents who make good decisions for you that would be considered a great favor. At the age where you begin making your own choices, you realize that they have laid some good foundation for your life by what they taught you, and by what they showed by their example.

People's experiences vary. There are people who are born to happy homes. Some are born into single-parent homes with many more challenges. There are people who do not know their fathers, for example, until several years later.

Worse still, there are people who are born out of traumatic situations like rape and they have to carry that sentiment throughout their growing years.

Whatever your situation, I have good news for you. In this life, it is not so much how it began that matters; it is how you end it. The truth is that how you end it is no longer in the hands of your parents. It is a matter between you and the God who allowed you to be born in the first place.

Most people start applying their power of choice when they attain the age of two. At that age however, all they know is, "No." They are so self-centered that anything they are asked to do meets the response, "No." As they grow, the power of choice becomes more mature, especially when they see the results of some decisions they make early in life. Simple truths like if you hit somebody he will hit you back, etc., begin to usher him or her into a new reality that choices have consequences. Even at that age, their minds are not mature enough to appreciate that fact. They still go around hitting people and getting hit back. It takes some time before the decision to hit someone is gradually brought under control.

From the time you are born into the world until the time you become of age to make your own decisions and become responsible for them, your life is almost entirely in the hands of your parents. In addition, by extension, mother and father figures, depending on your circumstances.

Let me remind you here, however, that it is at those stages of your life that the grace of God is available to you. You are often not aware that God is keeping you, but He surely does that.

Your background is very important, but it is not a trap forever, nor is it an absolute guarantee of what your life will become. Some people have very good backgrounds. They are born into rich, well-to-do families with everything going well for them; yet, their end is still sometimes very sad. Others may start life with all the troubles you can list; yet, they end very successfully.

Since God is always working for our good and He never leaves us to just anything, it holds true then, that the factor that often determines our success in life is the choices we make when we attain the age of responsibility.

Every person can look back into his life and at a point stop blaming his parents for situations where things have not gone well for him. We can always see a point where we had to make certain decisions and we made the wrong ones. It is often helpful if you stop blaming your parents or your early beginnings for your current troubles and start making some good decisions for your life.

2.

SEEK YOUR CREATOR
IN YOUR YOUTH

Seeking God early in life is considered the most important decision we can make using our power of choice. God wants each of us to have a meaningful life. He has a good plan for your life and that plan starts when you are born. The plan works like a partnership; there is a part that you play and there is a part that God plays as the Senior Partner. The most critical decision for any person is to know God early.

Read what the preacher wrote in Ecclesiastes, chapter 12

> [1] *Remember also your Creator in the days of your youth, before the evil days come and the years draw near of which you will say, "I have no pleasure in them";*
>
> [2] *before the sun and the light and the moon and the stars are darkened and the clouds return after the rain,*

³ *in the day when the keepers of the house tremble, and the strong men are bent, and the grinders cease because they are few, and those who look through the windows are dimmed,*

⁴ *and the doors on the street are shut—when the sound of the grinding is low, and one rises up at the sound of a bird, and all the daughters of song are brought low.*

Ecclesiastes 12:1-4

Why is it critical for you to seek your Creator while you are young? The most appropriate response to this question is that God holds your future. If God has a plan for your life, then it is in your interest to know Him early, so you do not miss that plan. Is it possible to miss God's plan for your life? Absolutely, yes!

Many people go through life doing a lot of trial and error, and by the time they find a clue to why they are here on earth, half of their given life on earth has passed.

Let me take you to a conversation that ensued between Jesus and one of the religious leaders of his day. Nicodemus came to Jesus by night, as we know the story. His foremost remark to Jesus was that he knew Jesus had come from above because no man could do the things He was doing if God were not with him.

Jesus told Nicodemus that except a man be born again he cannot see the kingdom of God. In other words, all people who are not born again are outside the kingdom of God. If you are out of the kingdom of God then you automatically find yourself in the kingdom of the devil. That is a simple non-debatable truth. Some people would not like it being said that openly and bluntly, but that is the truth.

That is the decision we are talking about here. What does it mean to be born again?

When you are born again, your spirit man is renewed. Your spirit is resurrected from the dead, literally. Your spirit is the means by which God communicates with you.

When Adam sinned, the human spirit almost died. It lost its ability to communicate with God. It lost its ability to receive from God the way God designed things to be. That explains why people get involved in all kinds of lifestyles. Their lives become subject to the power of sin and it manifests in several forms. The new birth that Jesus spoke about is what links you back to the Father as God's child.

The new birth does not come automatically. Everyone must decide that he wants to become born again. No one can force you to become born again. You have to decide on your own.

In order to redeem fallen humanity to Himself, God made the first move. He allowed His

Son to be made in our likeness so He would defeat the devil who had kept, and continues to keep, people in all kinds of bondage. Jesus destroyed the devil on our behalf so we can be saved and delivered from his chains and from bondage

> ¹⁴ *Since therefore the children share in flesh and blood, he himself likewise partook of the same things, that through death he might destroy the one who has the power of death, that is, the devil,*
>
> ¹⁵ *and deliver all those who through fear of death were subject to lifelong slavery.*
>
> ¹⁶ *For surely it is not angels that he helps, but he helps the offspring of Abraham.*
>
> ¹⁷ *Therefore he had to be made like his brothers in every respect, so that he might become a merciful and faithful high priest in the service of God, to*

make propitiation for the sins of the people.

¹⁸ For because he himself has suffered when tempted, he is able to help those who are being tempted

Hebrews 2:14-18

Jesus completed that great work on the cross but for it to become meaningful to anyone, that person must first make that decision I am referring to here. You must decide that you want Jesus to forgive you and deliver you from sin and the power of sin and make you God's child.

As many as received Jesus He gave them the power to become the children of God.

John 1:12

How does one get born again?

You do this by a simple prayer, asking God to forgive your sins by the blood of Jesus and asking Jesus to come and live in your heart

> *Behold, I stand at the door and knock. If anyone hears my voice and opens the door, I will come in to him and eat with him, and he with me*
>
> Revelation 3:20

This is the process to get born again:

1. Acknowledge that you are a sinner, born out of fallen Adam and Eve, helpless and unable to save yourself from sin and its effects.

2. Believe that Jesus Christ, God's only begotten Son, knew of your condition and came to die for your sins on the cross, and shed His blood for your redemption.

3. Believe that He rose from the dead to seal your salvation.

4. Pray and ask Jesus to forgive you as a sinner and the sins you have committed until this present day.

5. Specifically, ask Jesus to live in your heart as your Lord and Savior. In this prayer you are actually asking the Holy Spirit to live in your heart.

On the next page is the form of the prayer you pray to become born again:

Dear Lord,

I acknowledge that I am a sinner and cannot help myself. Your Word says that for my sins and trespasses Jesus was crucified on the cross, and that with His blood I am saved from the enemy. I believe that You are my Lord and Savior by Your death and resurrection. I open my heart to You now to come and live, just as You have indicated. Please forgive my sins and make me Your child, and I shall live for You the rest of my life.

In Jesus' name I pray,

Amen.

Anyone who prayed this prayer sincerely has become born again. When you pray this prayer an Old Testament prophet best captures what God does for you and to you:

²⁴I will take you from the nations and gather you from all the countries and bring you into your own land.

²⁵I will sprinkle clean water on you, and you shall be clean from all your uncleanness, and from all your idols I will cleanse you.

²⁶And I will give you a new heart, and a new spirit I will put within you. And I will remove the heart of stone from your flesh and give you a heart of flesh.

²⁷And I will put my Spirit within you, and cause you to walk in my statutes and be careful to obey my rules.

²⁸You shall dwell in the land that I gave to your fathers, and you shall be my people, and I will be your God

Ezekiel 36:24-28

God promised to give you His Spirit to make you strong. It means that you have something the ordinary young person does not have. Whereas they may be struggling trying to combat the pressures of growing up, you have strength from within, provided by the Holy Spirit. That places you at an advantage in the journey of life.

When you become a child of God early in life, you grow through your teen years with the grace of God abounding toward you.

That is where you make the right choices. That is when you can stand against all the pressures of the growing years. In your power you cannot do it. You need the power of God.

My name is

_____

[Name]

and I got born again on

_____

[Date]

3.

PURSUE GOD WITH ALL YOUR HEART

It is not enough to be born again. You must pursue God. To pursue something is to earnestly desire that thing to the point that all your activities in life are directed at getting that thing. The good thing is that God is more than anything you choose to pursue in this life. The pursuit of God will bring you manifold blessings you cannot imagine.

God's arms are open and His heart is also waiting for you. For every step you make towards God you can be sure that He has made more than 10 steps towards you. King David describes his pursuit after God in this Psalm:

> 1 *As a deer pants for flowing streams, so pants my soul for you, O God.*
>
> 2 *My soul thirsts for God, for the living God. When shall I come and appear before God?*
>
> 3 *My tears have been my food day and night, while they say to me all the day long, "Where is your God?"*

Psalm 42:1-3

Very early in life, every person must cultivate the pursuit of God. Do you see how King David describes the pursuit of God? He compares it to a deer that is looking for water. Until it finds water, it cannot stop. Just as that deer cannot live without water, constantly remind yourself that without God you cannot live.

God believes in young people. Remember he called Samuel at an early age and told him what He was about to do in Israel. God did not talk to Eli the high priest; he spoke to the young Samuel.

As a young growing person there are so many things that fight for your attention. It is understandable because most youth are actually in the process of discovering their world. This is the stage where they are hearing and seeing so many things they did not see or hear in the earlier years.

Those new things draw their attention often with equal magnitude. Each one presents itself as important and the young person is tempted to give them equal attention. That could be draining on the immature resources to deal with them. A lot of young people have not developed the ability to discern between what is helpful and what is not helpful. That explains the high level of experimentation that goes on in the youthful years. By the time they have made several experiments, they have also committed several errors, some very costly.

Whatever they find as important they end up pursuing with all their energy. This is the stage where young people must give attention to the pursuit of God. This is the time when their hunger and thirst for God should be ahead of every other passion.

Most youth channel their energy into gifts and talents and their development, which is positive, but the truth is that it takes quite some time for one to be fulfilled in whatever you find as your gift or talent. It is a process that takes years, and because youth usually want an immediate answer and immediate gratification and fulfillment, frustration can set in if they do not see immediately what they perceived to be coming very soon.

The pursuit of God provides the base or foundation even for the development of all other aspects of your life.

4.

DISCOVER YOUR PURPOSE

One of the advantages of knowing God early in your life is that you learn to discover your purpose at an early age. Read what God said concerning His plans and purposes for your life:

> *For I know the plans I have for you, declares the* LORD, *plans for welfare and not for evil, to give you a future and a hope.*

> Jeremiah 29:11

What this means is that instead of doing trial-and-error with your life, you can know very early what God wants you to do. People have all kinds of suggestions about how to know God's will for them, but the best is when God Himself ministers to you concerning that. Because most people are not properly guided to start with God early there is always a struggle because they cannot even know when God is saying something to them. You have the privilege of getting to that place as a young person if your pursuit of God is right on target.

Your purpose is the reason for which you were born. It comes to you as what you want to do with all your passion. It is something you will enjoy doing, even if you get no financial gains from it. (God has actually designed life so that pursuing your purpose will bring you prosperity, so you don't have to worry about money.)

I have described several statements below for you to consider. When you are walking through your day, observing things that happen around you, hearing what is happening around the world, which of these tug at your heart? To which of the scenarios below can you make the following statement?

For as long as God gives me life and health in this world...

a. *There will be no people around me struggling with health issues, fighting against all kinds of sicknesses and living hopelessly because they* cannot afford to take care of their health. No person in my world will die prematurely because his body could not sustain him. I see people living healthily all the time and that is what I want to believe God for.

b. Too many people live in dilapidated buildings and some even live in kiosks. My heart aches to see that happening. In my world, people will no longer struggle to have a roof over their head. Mud houses are a thing of the past, not in the 21st century. By the grace of God, I want to make sure people have a good roof over their heads always; one they can afford.

c. There will be justice on earth. I mean God's form of justice, and not the one where innocent people go to jail and the guilty ones walk free on the streets ready to commit more heinous crimes. The underprivileged in society will have a voice, children and women will no longer be downtrodden by the wicked of society. There will be a voice to defend the defenseless, and that voice will be mine.

d. People will no longer starve. God has given vast fertile lands and the wisdom to plant and harvest all man needs to feed himself. Food will abound for all in my world, and hunger will be totally eliminated.

e. Corruption will no longer become the order of the day. Those who vow to perpetuate all forms of corruption will have a hard time surviving wherever I find myself. They will be found, exposed, and feel regret for corrupting society. I will chase them out with every means that is available to me.

f. There will be no more sorrow in the hearts of people, no matter what they go through. They will receive what they need to cheer themselves up as they prepare to face other challenges that come their way. People should have a place where they can cry without fear of *being exploited, a place where they can be helped to grow and confront their issues.*

Clearly, you see that your purpose is not the particular job you want to do. For example, it is inaccurate to say that your purpose is to become a lawyer. What will make you want to be a lawyer is that you hate injustice with your guts and you want to do everything with the life and resources God gives you to fight injustice. That is what points you to the profession of a lawyer. The problem is that people choose the job they think is prestigious without the purpose for that profession. They are the ones who practice their profession anyhow, sometimes for the wrong reasons.

You can see why it is common to find teachers who exploit their students, nurses and doctors who kill in our hospitals, lawyers who set free the guilty, etc. They placed the job before the passion.

It is always right to check your heart and see your heartbeat before you even think of what occupation you should get in. If you follow your passion properly, you will then be energized to do whatever it demands to get engaged in that profession.

Whichever of these bubbles strongly in your heart defines your purpose. What follows from here is developing you and finding channels by which this can happen. It starts with discovering your seed.

My purpose in life is

_____

_____

_____

_____

_____

_____

5.

DISCOVER AND DEVELOP YOUR SEED

Your seed is the natural endowment that God has placed within you. That is what makes you unique. As you grow, it begins to show. Your seed is what makes you stand out in the crowd.

Discovering one's seed is one area of development where most people have limited understanding.

The natural scholars have tried to identify what makes people unique. They called it intelligence. For a long time people were classified as intelligent or non-intelligent. Comparisons were made as to who was more intelligent than the other.

The measures that were crafted to capture people's intelligence came with a lot of errors. One that was common then, was the intelligent quotient (IQ). People's uniqueness was identified by their IQ.

After a long time, one psychologist by the name of Howard Gardner decided that we should look at people's uniqueness in a different way. He proposed what he called *The Multiple Intelligences*.

He identified eight intelligences under his categorization, and proposed we should see people's uniqueness more in terms of which of the intelligence(s) they manifest.

See if you find which of Gardner's categories best describes you.

a. ***Verbal-Linguistic:*** The ability to use words and language. You can easily build and develop vocabulary and understand words correctly and your usage.

b. ***Logical-Mathematical:*** The capacity for drawing meaningful conclusions from observing and analyzing statements (inductive and deductive thinking and reasoning), as well as the use of numbers and the recognition of abstract patterns.

c. ***Visual-Spatial:*** The ability to visualize objects as they occur in space, hence you are able to create internal images and pictures –

manifesting in artistic designs, mapping, ability to locate places easily even places that are not familiar, etc.

d. ***Body-Kinesthetic:*** The wisdom of the body and the ability to control physical motion. Ability to coordinate parts of your body or whole body movements in meaningful ways – hands, legs, feet, upper body, lower body, combinations of upper and lower body.

e. ***Musical-Rhythmic:*** The ability to recognize tonal patterns and sounds, as well as sensitivity to rhythms and beats.

f. ***Interpersonal:*** The capacity for person-to-person communications and relationships. You find it easy to develop and maintain healthy relationships with people.

g. ***Intrapersonal:*** The spiritual, inner states of being, self-reflection, and awareness. You have true knowledge of who you are and understand yourself perfectly.

h. ***Naturalist intelligence:*** The ability to draw on features of the natural world to solve problems. You have an interest in natural elements, such as gardens, forests, mountains, etc.

His proposal is that we should stop comparing people with others and, instead, we find in which of these a person is strong in and in which he is less strong.

This to me is the closest anyone has come to discovering what God teaches us in His Word about our differences. God endowed each of us differently. Even within one particular domain, people show different levels of potential. Read what God told Moses when He instructed him to build the tent for the meeting place (Today we call it a temple):

¹ The LORD said to Moses,

² See, I have called by name Bezalel the son of Uri, son of Hur, of the tribe of Judah,

³ and I have filled him with the Spirit of God, with ability and intelligence, with knowledge and all craftsmanship,

⁴ to devise artistic designs, to work in gold, silver, and bronze,

⁵ in cutting stones for setting, and in carving wood, to work in every craft.

⁶ And behold, I have appointed with him Oholiab, the son of Ahisamach, of the tribe of Dan. And I have given to all able men ability, that they may make all that I have commanded you

Exodus 31:1-6

This is just an example of God saying how He has endowed some people. He made us different and we should, therefore, be looking for uniqueness in people.

These endowments are closely linked to your purpose. If your parents discover your seed earlier, they will be in position to get you into the right environment for the development of your seed as you prepare for life.

Natural endowments are closely linked to what one becomes in the future. So if discovery of the future comes early, then the rest of what you do becomes meaningful.

Out of these natural endowments come all the professions that are out there – musicians, architects, engineers, medical doctors, teachers, nurses, accountants, lawyers, pastors, etc. These career paths, as we call them today, are simply the opportunities to execute your purpose in life.

My Gardner category is closest to

_____

_____

_____

_____

_____

_____

Developing your seed through Education

When you discover your seed, it is just the beginning. You must find the most appropriate environments to nurture your seed. Nature itself is a spontaneous educational environment to develop your seed. Life itself has a way of preparing us to develop our natural endowments. In traditional settings, this is taken to the next level when people engage in apprenticeship. That is where they are discipled by someone who is considered an expert in that trade.

We all agree, however, that the common environment for many to develop their natural endowment is a formal school. Now, you have to understand that kindergarten to the university provides ample opportunity to develop your seed into skills that will enable you achieve your purpose. There are some people who may not go up to university, but life itself provides enough opportunity to develop their seed. Enrolling in a school has a way of speeding the process for many.

What this means is that while in school, you should pay attention to the opportunities made available in the school system to develop. Learning is not something to take lightly. If you don't commit to learning you will never develop your natural endowment. You will manage to pass exams, leave school, and still remain underdeveloped. It is a common experience that you don't want to have.

Going to school becomes more meaningful if you see the school as the avenue for the development of your natural endowment.

You cannot graduate from university, for example, and not know what you are going to do after that. Unfortunately, most people find themselves in such a situation.

Most young people who get frustrated after graduation got it wrong before entering university in the first place.

The education systems in most underdeveloped countries are so rigid and stereotyped that when one enters, it is difficult to make a detour and change course, even if they discover later they are in the wrong place. It amounts to a couple of years wasted and they force themselves to complete what they started. As a result, they come out and struggle.

That should never happen to you. While you are young, seek counsel and go through any process available that helps you unearth your natural endowments and get an idea of what your career path is likely to be.

Your career path, if properly discovered, is linked with God's purpose for your life.

6.

PURSUE YOUR PURPOSE

Career is a future thing, but it also starts early in your life. It is good for the young person to be certain of what he wants to do with his life when he feels he has had enough of education to prepare him. When you are out of school, the immediate path ahead of you is to pursue your purpose.

When you graduate from school the next thing you think about is work. This mentality is fueled by the fact that you are thinking about earning money. This is quite understandable. After all these years of schooling all you want to see is some money in your bank accounts.

With that in mind a lot of people forget to acknowledge career as the path of fulfilling the purpose they identified earlier. With this separation of career and purpose, most people deviate and sacrifice purpose for making money.

Whatever you choose as your purpose, your first day at work is actually the first day that you formally enter into the purpose. Career actually provides opportunity to execute your purpose. If the people who coined the word "career" had God's purpose in mind, they would have used different terminology. Today, if people say "career", it is more self-centered than God-centered.

If you understand that what you call your career is actually you fulfilling what God has called and prepared you to do, it will make a lot of difference. You do it not as unto man, but unto God and you always draw wisdom and guidance from the Holy Spirit to do it.

Some people who don't get it right before they enter university change after a few years of work when they have truly found their purpose, or rather found the right opportunity to execute their purpose for living.

The extent to which you will enjoy your career is determined by how prepared you are at the point of starting. That is why it is important to take education and training very seriously, because your life depends on it. Some think they are pursuing education because their parents asked them to, and by the time it is all over they see that they have robbed themselves of preparing for their life's purpose.

Understanding Careers in the Life Span

Donald E. Super's *Career Development Theory* is perhaps the most widely known life-span view of career development. Developmental theories recognize the changes that people go through as they mature, and they emphasize a life-span approach to career choice and adaptation. These theories usually partition working life into stages, and they try to specify the typical vocational behaviors at each stage.

He defined a career as a sequence of occupations, jobs, and positions held during the course of a lifetime, including also pre- and post-vocational activities.

Super and his colleagues outlined five major stages of career development, with each one characterized by three or four appropriate developmental tasks:

1. **Growth** (roughly ages 4 to 13) is the first life stage. This is the period when children develop their capacities, attitudes, and interests. They socialize their needs, and form a general understanding of the world of work. This stage includes four major career developmental tasks: (1) becoming concerned about the future; (2) increasing personal control over one's own life; (3) convincing oneself to achieve in school and at work; (4) and acquiring competent work habits and attitudes.

2. **Exploration** (ages 14-24) is the period when individuals attempt to understand themselves and find their place in the world of work. Through classes, work experience,

and hobbies, they try to identify their interests and capabilities and figure out how they fit with various occupations. They make tentative occupational choices and eventually obtain an occupation. This stage involves three career development tasks: (1) the crystallization of a career preference, is to develop and plan a tentative vocational goal; (2) the specification of a career preference, is to convert generalized preferences into a specific choice, a firm vocational goal; and (3) implementation of a career preference by completing appropriate training and securing a position in the chosen occupation.

3. **Establishment** (ages 25-44) is the period when the individual, having gained an appropriate position in the chosen field of work, strives to secure the initial position and pursue chances for further advancement.

This stage involves three developmental tasks: (1) stabilizing or securing one place in the organization by adapting to the organization's requirements and performing job duties satisfactorily; (2) consolidation of one's position by manifesting positive work attitudes and productive habits along with building favorable coworker relations; and (3) obtain advancement to new levels of responsibility.

4. **Maintenance** (ages 45-65) is the period of continual adjustment, which includes the career development tasks of holding on, keeping up, and innovating. The individuals strive to maintain what they have achieved, and for this reason they update their competencies and find innovative ways of performing their job routines. They try also to find new challenges, but usually little new ground is broken in this period.

5. **Disengagement** (over 65) is the final stage. It entails the period of transition out of the workforce. In this stage, individuals encounter the developmental tasks of deceleration, retirement planning, and retirement living. With a declined energy and interest in an occupation, people gradually disengage from their occupational activities and concentrate on retirement planning. In due course, they make a transition to retirement living by facing the challenges of organizing new life patterns.

Super's model demarcates the stages both with age bounds and task markers. Originally, Super viewed the stages as chronological, but later he also acknowledged an age-independent, task-centered view of stages. For example, individuals embarking on a new career in their middle adulthood might go through exploration and establishment stages. Thus, the five stages spreading across one's entire life span, or the "maxicycle," might also be experienced as "minicycles," within each of the maxicycle stages. Individuals cycle and recycle throughout their life span as they adapt to their own internal changes or to changed opportunities to which they are exposed.

Super assumed that not everyone progresses through these stages at fixed ages or in the same manner. This notion led him to develop and elaborate on the construct of career maturity (initially called vocational maturity), which denotes the readiness of the individual to make career decisions. Operationally, it is defined as the extent to which an individual has completed stage-appropriate career developmental tasks in comparison with other people of the same age.

Super and his colleagues devoted much effort to define this construct and develop appropriate measures. They identified five primary dimensions of vocational maturity: (1) "planfulness" or awareness of the need to plan ahead; (2) readiness for exploration; (3) informational competence (comprising knowledge about work, occupations, and life career roles); (4) decision-making skills; (5) and reality orientation. Super believed that a young person should be mature enough to benefit from career assessment and counseling. In adults, where recycling through career stages is less dependent on age, Super suggested that readiness for career decision making should be referred to as career adaptability.

7.

SETTLE FOR LIFE

Marriage and Family

Marriage is a major commitment. It makes a lot of sense and it is considered wise, to enter marriage when you have started your career. In other words, it is not advisable for someone who is not working to get married. We can glean from Scriptures that God gave Adam work to do before He gave him a wife, whom God called a helpmate. This is why if you find teenagers who are still in school talking about marriage you know immediately that they have not got it right.

The kind of marriage one cultivates has the potential to enhance the achievement of one's life goals or hinder it, and in some cases, completely overturn it.

The truth about marriage is that most people do not prepare for it. They assume that when they attain a certain age that marriage will happen. Yes, at a certain age people will be asking you if you intend to marry, and ask if you have found a partner or not. No one will ask you if you have prepared yourself for marriage.

It is interesting how of all the future issues, marriage, which is actually settling down for life with someone of the opposite sex, preoccupies young people, sometimes prematurely. The world has changed its standards and an issue of relationship with the opposite sex has become a nightmare. People get entangled with the wrong persons out of lust and inordinate affections. It is not uncommon to find a 17-year old who has had multiple breakups with the opposite sex. The word "love" has become something like a toy to play with, not considering its full implications.

Some young people actually put their future in jeopardy because of getting involved emotionally with the opposite sex too early.

Preparing for marriage is not the six months premarital counseling that people go through before they get married. If you have not developed within yourself all the qualities and attitudes that will make one have an enjoyable marriage, six months of premarital classes will make little or no difference.

At the youthful stages of life, it pays to develop healthy relationships with the opposite sex. This gives opportunity to learn about each other as one thinks of the future. It is not out of place if, toward the end of university education, one finds someone he intends to spend his life with, but it is not a must. And the person may not necessarily be someone from the university one attended. The rush to get hooked to someone before you leave the university places the whole marriage enterprise in jeopardy.

At this stage, it is enough to know about marriage, but not to attempt any of the lifestyles that lead to marriage.

1. Get knowledge and understanding about marriage – why God instituted it, who should

marry, and at what point in life it is most appropriate to consider the marriage option.

2. Learn about the characteristics you need to develop in other to marry properly. Just as you are spending four years for your first degree, and you spend another two years for your masters, and possibly five years for a doctorate, all before you consider yourself ready to practice your profession, give preparation for marriage the equivalent preparation.

3. Learn to understand the opposite sex because friendship within the same sex is different in many ways from friendship with someone of the opposite sex.

4. Develop the discipline of waiting for the most appropriate time to marry. If you rush into a relationship and start behaving like people who are married, you bring untold hardship upon yourself and create potential danger

against enjoying your marriage when it happens.

Belong to a good church and go through the process of preparing yourself for life. I believe that a good church will not just take youth through the tidbits of relationships, but provide discipleship that will help them develop the traits that will make them marry properly.

You have to understand at this point that marriage is not an opportunity to have sex with someone without feeling guilty about it. A lot of young people are only looking forward to the time when they can have sex and no one will complain about it.

Take time to develop character. If you have not learned how to discipline your emotions, for example, you will marry and still be looking at other women who look more beautiful than your wife. That is where trouble starts.

If you have not developed self-control, you will always be fighting with your spouse over little things. If you have not learned the art of being faithful, you easily slip into adultery and destroy what potentially can be a happy marriage for you. Don't underestimate the process of preparing yourself and don't rush into marriage.

8.

PREPARE YOUR LEGACY AND EXIT

Legacy

Legacy has to do with what you are leaving behind after death. Most people do not plan to die. When I talk about planning to die I am not referring to planning to commit suicide. I mean getting ready such that when your time comes you can say that you have lived well. A lot of people get frustrated in their later years on earth because they feel they have failed in this life.

They struggle to find what positive contributions they have made to life and they find none. Some who did not go through the stages thoroughly and well, end up having miserable experiences in their mature years before they pass on.

The way to avoid becoming frustrated in your latter years is to ask the questions that the mature ask, but much earlier. At age 60, most people will be asking themselves the following questions: *What have I done with my life? What am I leaving behind for the next generation? What impact have I made in the lives of the people I gave birth to, or the young people who knew me? What have I achieved in my life?*

If the person is deeply religious, he will be asking what answer he is going to give to God who gave him life and all the opportunities that came his way. Now they reflect on how many opportunities came their way and they blew it. If they think they did well, they live the rest of their mature years in peace and in excitement. If they think they have failed in life, they go through that last lap of their life very frustrated.

The young person avoids all these by asking the questions now and not later. What do I want to do with my life? How do I want to be remembered when I leave this life? What impact do I want to make in life and in the people that come my way in this life? What account will I give to God who gave me life and blessed me with a great talent?

If you start thinking of what you want to leave for the generations after you, then you can work towards it. Is it a book you want to write? Is it an instrument you want to create for use in a medical practice? Is it pieces of music that will lift people up spiritually and establish them emotionally? Is it a new way of doing something that no one has thought of?

These are questions that should be asked while you are still young and in school preparing for your purpose. If you do that, it is possible to even start working on what you think is your legacy for the generation after you.

Exit

The last thing that happens to every man is death. That brings your life on earth to an end. God has appointed that every man born of Adam will die. This is what we brought upon ourselves at the beginning of creation in the Garden of Eden through

Adam. When Adam disobeyed God, he brought in death, which is twofold.

First there is the spiritual death. When Adam disobeyed God he did not die physically. He immediately died spiritually. It means he lost the consciousness of God that God gave him.

Spiritual death is actually separation from God. This separation blocks our ability to communicate effectively with God. That explains why we struggle today to know and understand God and His ways.

Second, there is the physical death, which is the cessation of existence on earth. Later, Adam died physically and people have continued to die physically up to the present.

The announcement I have for you today is that one day after you have lived long on earth and become old and probably cannot do much in life again, you are going to go. That is the last stage for everyone born of Adam.

The Bible says, however, that after this death we will one day face God's judgment. This has to do with how we lived our lives on earth. It is interesting to note that the preacher drew the attention of young people to this fact. The preacher did not wait for people to become old before talking about the judgment that awaits all people after death.

This is what he wrote to young people:

> *Rejoice, O young man, in your youth, and let your heart cheer you in the days of your youth. Walk in the ways of your heart and the sight of your eyes. But know that for all these things God will bring you into judgment.*

> Ecclesiastes 11:9

Later in the Scriptures, the writer of Hebrews also mentioned the judgment this is what he also wrote:

²⁷ And just as it is appointed for man to die once, and after that comes judgment,

²⁸ so Christ, having been offered once to bear the sins of many, will appear a second time, not to deal with sin but to save those who are eagerly waiting for him.

Hebrews 9:27-28

God wants you very early in life to know and understand that one day you will give account of your life to Him. It is not supposed to put fear in you; it is meant to make you aware. If you go to the doctor and he tells you if you do not eat good food you will die before your time, he is not putting fear in you. He is only informing you of what could be so you can take good care of yourself.

In the same way God wants you to know as early in life as possible, that there is a day of accountability for every man. It is just like the examiner gives you the syllabus for the exam so you can study and not fail the exam. Without the syllabus you may study things that are not required for that particular exam and may fail through no fault of yours. God is fair so He is telling you as a youth that one day you will answer for the things you looked at, the things you allowed to occupy your heart, the things you got involved in, the things that became your passion throughout your life, and the things you pushed everything aside to pursue. Whatever they were, whether good or bad, you will be giving account of them.

9.

REFLECTION OF THE STAGES OF LIFE

Two of the stages of life are very much out of your control. We all know that the first is birth to your parents. No one chooses his parents and when or where they should be born. You may be born in a manger like the baby Jesus. You may be born in a rich hospital or a small midwifery in a village somewhere. The truth is that this makes little difference in terms of your total life and what you are going to become.

The second is death, your exit from this earth. You have no control over your death. With good nutrition and exercise and taking good care of yourself, you can extend your normal lifespan, but no matter how hard and how good you are at this, one day you will give up.

The Scriptures suggest that each man is entitled to at least 70 years. Every man must strive to hit 70 and ask for more. God will grant it. God does not kill people because they have attained 70. Some have lived in this present time to be 90, 95, or even 100. Nevertheless, you will die. It is out of your hand.

The stages in between are more than 100% in your hands. No one can make the decision to accept Jesus Christ as Lord and Savior for you. You have to make it yourself, just like no one drinks medicine for a sick person. Once you make that decision, continuing to pursue God and have fellowship with him is also upon you. Many, after they have made the decision to let Jesus save them from their sins, refuse to continue to have meaningful fellowship with Him.

The result is that they do not enjoy Christian life as they should. It ends up being an up and down life; today they are up, tomorrow they are down. Today they feel they are Christians, and tomorrow they feel they have never been born again.

The first few stages follow an order: birth; seeking God; and pursuing God. The rest of them are not chronological as such. What you need to do is to sit down and reflect over your life again. See exactly at which stage you are predominantly and how you are doing, whether great or you need to do better. See also which stages are happening concurrently and what each contributes to the other.

You have to learn to be in charge of your life at any point in time. When you do that, you free yourself of several distractions in the name of peer pressure. I will address peer pressure in this series of booklets meant to prepare you to face life.

When you maintain your focus in the face of peer pressure, you grow into the fine young man or woman God intends you to become. Then, you progress to adult life and continue to fulfill your purpose before you die.

N. Duncan-Williams' Declaration for You

- I declare that the favor of God will be upon you everywhere you go.

- As you navigate the stages of life, you will find God at every point.

- I activate the anointing of God upon your life.

- God will lead you to take your territories even as a young person.

- In this time of your life, I declare that nothing shall stand in your way.

- Nothing will be able to knock you off God's plan and purpose for your life.

- You will walk in your highways and follow God's plan for your life.

- You shall be a light to your generation.

- They shall come and learn from you.

I want you to take hold of this declaration and make them your own. Say them to yourself and to your situation and see the power of God begin to work on your behalf.

Amen!!!

My Personal Declaration

1.

2.

3.

4.

5.

6.

7.

8.

9.

www.ingramcontent.com/pod-product-compliance
Lightning Source LLC
Chambersburg PA
CBHW071816020426
42331CB00007B/1496